For Your Garden
SEATS AND BENCHES

For Your Garden
SEATS AND BENCHES

CAROL SPIER

Little, Brown and Company
Boston   New York   Toronto   London

First Edition

ISBN 0-316-80834-2

Library of Congress Catalog Card Number 93-85926

A FRIEDMAN GROUP BOOK
10 9 8 7 6 5 4 3 2 1
Published simultaneously in Canada by Little, Brown & Company (Canada) Limited

FOR YOUR GARDEN: SEATS AND BENCHES
was prepared and produced by
Michael Friedman Publishing Group, Inc.
15 West 26th Street
New York, New York 10010

Editor: Kelly Matthews
Art Directors: Jeff Batzli and Lynne Yeamans
Designer: Stan Stanski
Photography Director: Christopher C. Bain

Color separations by Fine Arts Repro House Co., Ltd.
Printed and bound in China by Leefung-Asco Printers Ltd.

Table of Contents

INTRODUCTION

꧁ ꧂

Gardens, whether large or small, filled with lawns and shrubs, flower beds and borders, or rows of herbs and vegetables, provide the natural settings for homes. They offer protection from neighbors as well as a means of integrating homes into neighborhoods. Gardens are created to be admired by passersby and enjoyed by owners. They may be planted with their bounty in mind or designed to provide a fair-weather living space, but whether more time is spent caring for gardens or relaxing in them, all garden lovers are glad to find a place to pause and sit amid the beauty.

An important element in garden design, garden furniture should enhance the landscaping and should be selected with the same attention given to the plantings. It is equally important, however, to choose practical seating that suits your needs. Are you looking for true comfort or for a place to catch your breath? Do you wish to sit in the open or in shelter? Will the seat allow you to take advantage of a view or be the focus of one? Do you want to recline, read, or dine? Should your seating be stationary, or will you want to move it about? And lastly, your garden furniture should please your fancy.

INTEGRATING SEATS AND BENCHES WITH YOUR LANDSCAPE

Seats and benches placed within a garden invite outdoor relaxation. The style of garden furniture you select should be in keeping with the style of your garden— and with the architecture of your home if they will be viewed together. The more formal your landscaping, the more formal your seats and benches are likely to be; conversely, the more naturalistic the setting, the more rustic you may wish your furnishings. Gardens, like interiors, should be furnished with pieces that are in proportion to the space they will occupy, that complement and enhance the mood and style of the environment and the occupants. That being said, bear in mind that gardens are living and constantly changing places, and the history of garden design is filled with contrivance, conceit, and folly where humans have successfully inserted as many surprises as nature. As long as you understand the attitude you wish your garden to embody, you should feel free to trust your instincts and choose seats or benches that beckon you.

As you think about what sort of garden seating to select, consider whether your seats and benches will be prominent features of your landscape or tucked into intimate settings. Will they be adjacent to other structural elements—walkways, patios, arbors, walls, or even buildings—or set among trees, lawns, or borders? Also, don't neglect the changing of the seasons as you choose the material or color of your furnishings—be sure you will like them once flowers and foliage have faded. There are countless charming garden seats and benches to choose from—all with various maintenance requirements and, of course, varying costs, which will no doubt also influence your choice.

OPPOSITE: The airy white bench in this formal garden has a sprightly, upright attitude very much in keeping with the standard fruit trees it faces. The scrolled and woven metal is reminiscent of an elegant eighteenth-century bird cage, and although decorative enough to be important in this space, the bench is delicate and neither obscures nor overpowers the plantings.

ABOVE: Simple, gently curved stone benches mark the perimeter of this formal clearing, inviting the stroller to sit, enjoy the sun, and contemplate the garland-carrying statue. Stone is a classic material for garden ornament; it weathers well and quickly assumes an aspect of antiquity that is prized by many landscape designers—which is most appropriate to this setting.

RIGHT: The rustic stone bench in the middle of this backyard garden is simplicity itself and suits the shingled New England home behind it. The dwarf Alberta spruce trees that flank the gray bench will provide a green accent when the country flowers die back, giving the bench definition in wintertime.

OPPOSITE: This brick cottage is delightfully overgrown with climbing roses that transform its facade into a vertical garden. A weathered wood chair sits by the stoop, complementing perfectly the aged door and window. A visitor calling when no one is at home might choose to wait and perhaps drowse peacefully in perfumed sunlight.

ABOVE: Garden seats are often strategically placed to offer repose or a view at the end of a walk or prospect. Here, a classic Lutyens bench beckons at the end of a rose bower.

LEFT: The small glade of trees at the end of this large country lawn shelters a formal cast iron bench, which is a surprising contrast to the unpretentious setting but so charming and inviting as it comes into view.

OPPOSITE: Here, a circular drive skirts a spot of lawn covered by a bower of blooming fruit trees. Rustic twig benches sit informally below, catching the spirit of the branching limbs; later in the season, they will offer a casual and shady outdoor respite from the hot sun.

ABOVE: Providing a colorful edge to a lawn or terrace, perennial borders are usually admired and strolled past. An inviting bench has been tucked discreetly into this one, offering a fragrant spot to read, repose, or watch a game being played on the lawn.

OPPOSITE: Soon to be a vine-covered arbor, this formal green bench sits at the end of a tailored lawn that serves as a patio. The arch of the arbor repeats in the back of the bench.

ABOVE: Lest anyone forget, gardens are workplaces as well as showplaces, and you will probably be glad to have a resting place when planting, pruning, weeding, or harvesting yours. A carved wood bench is a welcome fixture in this walled New Mexican garden—a good choice in the terra-cotta-colored Spanish ambiance.

LEFT: When designing your landscape, consider creating a small garden around a bench. Here, a built-in seat embraces assorted stone pavings and is in turn framed with effusive cosmos and small potted bamboo. The mood is somewhat oriental and the effect much more interesting than a plot of flowers cut into the lawn.

ABOVE: Given some thought, found objects can be fashioned into garden seating in a formal landscape. This weathered plank resting on mossy stones beside a graveled path appears to have grown here; its grays and greens, rounds and flats meld harmoniously with the setting.

OPPOSITE: Wonderful chairs and benches can sometimes be discovered in the landscape, creating naturalistic and unobtrusive informal garden seating. A fallen branch may offer the perfect resting spot, as on this hillside where a large curved limb has been leveled with stones.

Chapter One

SITING SEATS AND BENCHES

If you are thinking about adding a chair or bench to your garden, your first consideration will probably be its location. The setting you choose for your furniture will most likely influence your choice of its style or design. While the site may be dictated by special needs such as offering a resting place along a long path or providing a spot to sit back out of the sun in a working garden, the location of garden furniture is more likely to be a matter of aesthetics, giving focus to a special feature—a view, a pool, a clearing or court, or an intimate spot—and allowing you to take advantage of it. Once you know where you want to place your chair, you will be able to decide how many people it should accommodate, if it should be built-in or movable, and what material, shape, and color it should be to best enhance the setting.

FOR A LONG VISTA

If your garden offers a prospect—a scenic view of sunrise or sunset, of neighboring woods, water, or meadows, or even of your own fairly large lawn, you will no doubt want to be able to sit down to enjoy it in comfort.

ABOVE: In a pastoral setting with a breathtaking view such as this, a rough-hewn slab bench is unobtrusive and inviting. While almost any bench would suit this lovely spot, there is something particularly appealing about one that owes little to the hand of man. You might, however, prefer a structure with a back so that you could lean back and relax.

OPPOSITE: This rolling country lawn has been broken up with interior hedges and flower beds that give it a sense of accessibility in spite of its large area. Benches placed within each section offer both long and short views and the possibility of sun or shade.

ABOVE: Benches tucked into the plantings at the edge or corner of a large lawn will appear and feel much more intimate than those set out in the open, even though they offer a wide prospect of the landscape and are in full view.

BY THE WATERSIDE

Water in a garden is an enticing, beckoning feature. It catches the light, moves with the wind, and reflects its surroundings; it may be natural or man-made, still or moving, planted or swimmable, but it is always fascinating. Whether you have a fountain, a lily pond, a reflecting pool, a meandering stream, or a sparkling cascade, you should be able to relax and dream beside it in comfort, so place an inviting seat nearby.

ABOVE: It would be difficult to resist basking in the sunlight at the edge of this lovely lily pond. Although one half of the pond is bordered with mature shrubbery, the prospect across the yard is open and might be spoiled by a heavy or self-important piece of furniture; this classic park bench is perfectly balanced with the site and sits in graceful repose, inviting company.

ABOVE: A bench built to encircle a tree trunk can be almost as magical as water, so what better choice for relaxing by a woodland pond? This one, designed with simple but thoughtful detail, has weathered nicely into its natural setting.

RIGHT: Fanciful wire-backed chairs sit in delicate contrast to a stone-framed pond. Unoccupied, their delicate tracery appears vinelike against the boulders.

ABOVE: Here, a simple stone slab perched atop stone supports blends with the organic edge that frames this goldfish pond. Ferns, flowers, and fish abound in this quiet nook.

AS A FOCAL POINT

Strategically placed seats and benches can be used to call attention to an important feature or area of your garden—or to create one. Use them to draw the eye, as well as the body, toward a specimen planting, a patio, a turn in a walkway, or a distant corner.

ABOVE: You need not start with a large parklike space nor an enticing natural feature to create an elegant garden. This yard has been thoughtfully enclosed and planned with simple but effective formality. The regularity of the design leads the eye to the central slate terrace, where a group of wicker chairs is ready for friendly discourse.

RIGHT: This aged and magnificent tree stands importantly in the center of a large and open lawn. While the eye is drawn in wonder to the tree's girth, the clean white bench encircling the trunk begs you to wander over for a closer look.

ABOVE: Paths in gardens large and small must lead somewhere—even if only to the property line. A bench viewed at the end of a path gives importance to the walk ahead. Here, a mown grass path leads irresistibly to an elegant and cleverly designed seat.

OPPOSITE: If you have a country estate large enough to offer the prospect of a distant seat, then place it where it can be seen from a porch or window. Here, a wonderful cast iron bench beckons you to rest under the honeysuckle and roses in the corner of a walled lawn.

AS A RETREAT

If your garden includes an intimate bower, a hidden nook, or an out-of-the-way clearing, furnish and use it as a private retreat—for reading, bird-watching, sketching, or tea—whenever weather permits.

ABOVE: A glade lost deep in a woodland garden is the perfect spot for quiet repose or close observation of any small inhabitants who might venture into the dappled light.

ABOVE LEFT: Espaliered fruit trees flank the entry to a wonderful green room, carpeted with lawn, walled with shrubbery, and overhung with leafy boughs. A table and chairs tucked at one end suggest open-air dining and private conversation.

OPPOSITE: Here, sitting picturesquely, a solitary chair is nearly lost amid masses of purple and green. While this bower will provide a summer-long shady retreat, it is in full and fragrant glory while the wisteria blooms overhead.

AS A RESPITE

While garden seats are often placed to take advantage of some landscape feature, you might have a more prosaic reason for siting one: you may simply need a place to rest when gardening. If you spend a lot of time tending your landscape or if your terrain is rough or hilly, then place a bench where it can offset your labor.

ABOVE & RIGHT: This combination cold frame and bench may be the ultimate in raised-bed gardening. It is convenient, practical, and attractive, and anyone with basic carpentry skills should be able to customize something similar.

OPPOSITE: Too much sun can be just as debilitating to the gardener as too much bending, pulling, or digging. If you've no room for a gazebo or pergola, you might consider a covered bench. A basket shelter such as this can also be moved to face away from the sun as needed.

ABOVE: Here, a more formal covered chair is like a tiny garden house, providing shelter from the sun or a gentle rain.

RIGHT: If a long stairway or steep path leads from one part of your yard to another, a bench situated along the way will let you catch your breath. On man-made stairs, repeat the building material for the bench; if you'll be climbing a natural path, you might prefer a fallen log or something more organically shaped.

ON A DECK OR TERRACE

If you have a deck or terrace in your garden, there are several factors that will influence the seating you choose. Is the terrace frequently used as an outdoor living or dining room? Does it focus on a view or border a pool? Is it adjacent to the house? Is it partially walled or covered or approached by steps? Are there potted plants or garden beds on it, or is the landscaping only on the perimeter? The seats and benches that make your terrace comfortable should complement as many of these factors as are present, so keep them in mind as you consider whether the seating should be wood, stone, or metal, movable or built-in, formal or naturalistic.

ABOVE: Slab-sided walls frame the shady terrace adjacent to this cottage. The benches that flank the wonderful potted hydrangea are of fittingly simple slab construction; they quietly welcome and offer rest.

LEFT: This walled terrace with its terra-cotta pavement and interior wood framing gives the appearance of an open-air home. Indeed, the residents use it that way whenever possible, dining and relaxing within the small "rooms."

ABOVE: Here, rustic twig armchairs seem at home under the twisted branches above and are easy to move about to take advantage of the fountain or the view through the gateway.

ABOVE: This marvelous tiled terrace sits like a small stage in lush green shrubbery. Tiled benches were built formally along the sides, but they are too far apart for easy conversation and must be supplemented with other chairs.

ABOVE: Backless stone benches are the perfect choice for this flagstone terrace, where they blend with the low wall, pavement, and tree trunk and allow you turn your gaze and face any direction you please.

OPPOSITE: Here, a perennial border provides a homey sense of place to a small deck perched on the edge of open countryside. Although the vantage point is spectacular, the rustic twig benches seem to grow easily out of the simple weathered planking; the overall effect is natural and unaffected.

Chapter Two

SITTING IN STYLE
AN OVERVIEW OF DESIGN STYLES AND MATERIALS

he design of a seat or bench completes the mood of a garden; its shape and material establish character, which will intrude, subtly or otherwise, upon the setting. The styles of garden furnishings are practically endless, ranging from straightforward, prosaic, and elegant to imaginative, charming, and whimsical. Many designs are traditional and are available in high-quality reproductions from specialty vendors, and most new garden furniture is made from durable—though not necessarily maintenance-free—materials.

Do consider seating comfort—neither charm nor elegance is synonymous with ease. Most garden seats are uncushioned so that they will be weatherproof; if you want the comfort of padding, be sure that cushions will look appropriate on the style of seat you choose, and be prepared to keep them out of the rain. In addition to deciding the style of your garden seating, you will also need to consider the size of each piece (single, double, or greater occupancy) and whether built-in or freestanding furnishings best suit your needs.

FREESTANDING SEATS

Freestanding seats and benches can be moved about as your needs change, but if you plan to move them frequently, be sure to consider their weight. Perhaps a greater advantage to freestanding seating is that you can purchase it ready-made; built-in seating is usually custom made. While stone furniture is durable enough to place directly on the ground, wood and metal will last longer if you set them on some sort of paving, and a small bed of brick or pebbles placed under the legs will protect them from rot—and keep slender feet from sinking into the earth.

OPPOSITE: Carved stone benches are traditionally associated with Renaissance garden design and are frequently seen in formal gardens. Because stone melds with its setting as it ages, it can be just as suitable in naturalistic gardens. Here, a charming little stool perches like a bit of raised pavement in this casually arranged and planted garden.

ABOVE: Cast iron garden furniture, which first became popular during the Victorian era, is available in all sorts of elegant and fanciful designs that often incorporate naturalistic motifs. Depending upon the particular design and locale, it can look truly sophisticated or charmingly tongue-in-cheek. This chair, with its painted patina, masquerades as an archaic construction of grapevine and acanthus.

ABOVE: The proportions of this gracefully curved wood bench are more massive than they might at first appear, but the bench is quiet, elegant, and serene in a large, open setting.

LEFT: For a discreet offer of repose, tuck a plain bench into a soft summer border. This untreated slab has mellowed through the years to sit unobtrusively on a hillside of blooms.

ABOVE: Even a simple wood bench can have elegant proportions; one such as this is quite straightforward, but the shaped planks give it an unexpected finesse.

LEFT: The wood-and-wrought-iron park bench is a classic, seen with minor variations throughout the Western world. It is at home in almost any situation, becoming more or less conspicuous as the environment varies from open to overgrown. Readily available bistro chairs provide a single-seat alternative to this style of bench, but they are not as comfortable for lounging.

OPPOSITE: Sturdy, slatted wood benches, which are often made of farmed teak, are widely available in a variety of formal and informal designs. Because they are so substantial, they can overpower a delicate or tiny garden, but they will complement an open or expansive setting or a substantial wall or hedge.

ABOVE: Humor need not be out of place in the garden. Here, an old plow has been amusingly transformed into a colorful and sunny bench.

RIGHT: Just as fallen tree trunks beckon woodland strollers to stop and sit, these thoughtfully but roughly hewn seats offer a natural resting spot at the edge of a yard—a charming way to redress a storm-felled tree.

OPPOSITE: Rustic twig furniture is most at home in unpretentious settings. This bench grows easily between the green lawn and a soft swath of blue, its lattice back paying wry homage to a more formal and classic bench design.

ABOVE: Rattan and wicker are good choices for sheltered garden seating, as on the portico next to this lovely kitchen garden—an inviting spot for breakfast or tea. These comfortable chairs are lightweight, making them easy to move out of inclement weather.

RIGHT: Lounge furniture is somehow neither as elegant nor as charming as its upright counterparts, but it may bring you closer to truly enjoying your garden. There is an age-old link between grape arbors and reclining; this garden provides a wonderful setting for an afternoon of relaxation.

BUILT-IN SEATS

If you are considering built-in seating for your garden, let the specifics of the setting guide the design of the furnishings. If your garden is formal, your built-in seating should be formal as well; if the setting is naturalistic, you should work with the elements at hand so your seating appears to have grown along with the vegetation. If you are using fences, arbors, or other architectural embellishments, your benches should repeat or complement their design—or be integral with them; if there are natural features such as rocks, stones, or logs, consider using them as construction material.

ABOVE & RIGHT: In rocky hillside environments, you can take advantage of the terrain by building a bench into a bank of earth and stone, then planting the crevices and allowing the whole to grow into a rock garden.

OPPOSITE: Rough timbers can be used instead of stones to create a naturalistic banquette. This one is stepped along a gently sloping lawn where, over time, it has weathered to harmonize with the rocky hillside behind it.

ABOVE: You need not have the excuse (or the ambition) of a stone wall to build a rustic stone bench. This one sits at the edge of a clearing, charmingly overgrown with ivy and morning glories.

ABOVE: If you are building a stone wall somewhere on your property, incorporate a place to sit at a strategic point. This slab-topped bench has a fern-filled planter at each end.

ABOVE: Brick is often used to trim both formal and informal gardens; it is readily available, inexpensive, and easy to work with. Here, a tailored bench sits at the end of a brick-lined pebbled pathway; it uses a heavy plank for its seat.

RIGHT: In a striking setting, understatement may be the key to a well-designed bench. Here, a grassy hillside rolls down to meet a curving pathway and a simple semicircular bench fills a niche carved where the path turns to enter a wood. The harmony of the repeated curves emphasizes the striking transition in the landscape.

BELOW: This lovely little bench is part of a formal terrace railing. It is nearly as delicate as its freestanding cousins and adds a flourish at the end of the railing.

OPPOSITE: Garden arbors filter the strong light of the sun and offer a bit of privacy, making them likely spots for lingering. Benches built inside will always be enticing, and this one, the focal point at one end of a clearing, features high-backed deep-set benches for extra seclusion.

ABOVE: Working gardeners as well as strollers need a place to rest. If you have permanent raised beds in your kitchen garden, think of rimming them with simple plank benches—planting, weeding, and harvesting will be easier. Be sure the benches are steady enough to walk on, so that you'll be able to spade and hoe without fear of tipping over.

SWINGS AND HAMMOCKS

Who can resist the gentle rocking of a hammock or the idle swaying of a garden swing? In daylight or moonbeam, you can escape, dally, linger, or forget, lulled by their drowsy passage, back and forth or side to side, to nowhere.

ABOVE TOP: A shade-blessed hammock with an eye toward a beautiful landscape is a great reward for hours of dirt-intensive labor. If your garden is as lush as this one, you should relax and revel in the view.

ABOVE: Discovering that two mature trees are the perfect distance apart can easily create an urge to indulge in some fresh-air repose. Should you wish to dress the set, you might embellish the trunks with boxes of flowers when you string up the hammock.

ABOVE: A classic porch swing will give as much pleasure under a tree as on a veranda. Pick a tree with a sturdy overhanging branch, and then enjoy its cool shade in summer and the warm sun in spring and autumn.

LEFT: A high branch, two strong cables, a smooth plank seat, and a good clear lawn are all the young-at-heart need to send fancy flying. Unless you are truly too sedate to indulge in an occasional moment on a swing, be sure that any single-seater you install is broad enough and strong enough to give you—and not just a child—a boost.

Chapter Three

CONSIDERING SHAPE, COLOR, AND PROPORTION

As you choose seating for your garden, your first thoughts will probably be about location and style, but shape, color, and proportion also influence the success with which a bench or chair sits in its environment. You select plants for the way their colors contrast or harmonize and their shapes create line and texture, and you should select garden furnishings with the same thoughts in mind. You may get the most use from your garden seats when the days are at their longest, but you will very likely look upon them all year long, so as you choose them, don't neglect to consider the changing seasons and the way the balance of shape, color, and proportion will be altered as the foliage comes and goes around them.

Green, white, and occasionally black are the classic color choices to impose on garden furnishings. Otherwise, wood, stone, and some metals can be sealed for protection or left to weather naturally. Bright colors may look wonderful in the right spot, but they are attention grabbers. The scale of your bench will be maximized or minimized by the contrast or intensity of its color against its setting—a heavy bench painted white will probably appear more important than the same bench painted dark green.

ABOVE: A park bench placed on a strip of lawn contrasts with a swath of brilliant spring colors, but because the bench is delicate and there is so much green around, the contrast is harmonious. Later in the season, this bench will blend into the bushes.

OPPOSITE: A painted-green bench will harmonize with shrubbery, contrasting gently with the foliage as leaves mature or dapple in the sunlight. This substantial bench stands out just enough to be apparent but does not startle or conflict with the bushes massed around it.

ABOVE TOP: A white bench set against shrubbery makes a cool but arresting contrast. The formality of this metal settee is emphasized by the grand potted white daisies at each arm.

ABOVE: You might expect to find Mistress Mary tripping lightly down the paths between these small but profusely planted beds, and these fanciful cast iron seats tucked into the far corner would make a charming resting spot for her.

RIGHT: The green-gray color of this prettily carved bench is an apt choice for this romantic and unusual setting, where it helps the eye make a flowery transition from rock to foliage.

ABOVE: A cast-stone fountain is the focus of this lovely sunken garden, which is paved with tiles made of the same material interspersed with creeping ground covers. The cast-stone bench at the far end is a perfect choice here, and the continuous ecru tone contrasts simply but starkly with the bright color and lush green of the borders—particularly attractive when the warm sun lights the spot.

OPPOSITE: This wonderful little seat seems to have been fashioned by the same hand that shaped the adjacent hedges. The color gray has a cooling effect, particularly when juxtaposed with green, and can be most welcome in warm weather.

ABOVE: Naturally weathered wood tends to gray with age, making it a good choice for a silver-toned garden such as this, where stone paving and blue-green foliage combine to make a monochromatic background that enhances the intensity of the massed lavender blooms.

OPPOSITE: As long as its shape and proportion are appropriate to the landscape, a weathered or clear-finished wood bench is likely to complement any garden. Essentially natural—even though contrived—wood furnishings tend to ride out the changing seasons with grace.

ABOVE: The square lattice back of this small bench is a nice complement to the grid of the brick wall behind it. Although this garden tends to be bleak in the off-season, there is something magical in the way the frost dusts each branch, stalk, and crevice—and the weathered gray of the bench—with silver.

LEFT: Autumn brings a new glory to a wooded garden, showering lawn and furnishings with brilliant color. A substantial wood or stone bench will hold its own in such an expansive setting—whether the season be green, russet, or barren.

ABOVE & RIGHT: There is nothing like a quilt of pristine snow for transforming a familiar garden into mysterious and larger-than-life scenery. Benches, like bushes and branches, will catch and hold the flakes; the broader and more numerous the surfaces, the more interesting the effect.